THE OFFICIAL
QUEENS PARK
RANGERS
ANNUAL 2012

Written by Francis Atkinson & Ian Taylor

Designed by Cavan Convery

A Grange Publication

© 2011. Published by Grange Communications Ltd., Edinburgh under licence from Queens Park Rangers Football Club.

Printed in the EU.

Photographs © Queens Park Rangers

ISBN: 978-1-908221-32-2

£7.99

Contents

Editor's Welcome...

The 2010/11 season will forever live long in the hearts of the QPR faithful.

The R's stormed to the npower Championship title, with memorable wins in the run-in over Leicester City (h), Reading (a) and Barnsley (a) helping seal the coveted crown.

In this annual, we take a look back at all the magic moments from the campaign, highlighting some of the great goals and games, as well as paying tribute to those people that made it happen.

We've got crosswords and wordsearches and much, much more. So sit back, relax and savor everything that was special about 'the season of all seasons' at Loftus Road!

Come on you R's!

QUEENS
PARK
RANGERS

LOFTUS ROAD · LONDON · 1882

Season Review 2011-12

**It was the moment all QPR fans had been waiting for...
Rangers are back in the Premier League!**

After a 15 year absence from the top-flight, the Hoops sealed
their place back in the world's top domestic league thanks to a
remarkable season for Neil Warnock's men.

Here, we pay tribute to the people that made the dream become
a reality, as we look back at all the games, goals, thrills and spills
that made this season one to remember...

August

The R's got the ball rolling on their title-winning campaign thanks to a magnificent start in the opening month.

Goals from Heidar Helguson, Jamie Mackie, Adel Taarabt and Fitz Hall sealed a 4-0 win over Barnsley on the opening day of the season and, despite a disappointing exit in the First Round of the Carling Cup against Port Vale at Loftus Road, QPR rounded off the month with a further seven points from a possible nine.

Neil Warnock's men brushed aside former Club Sheffield United in stunning style with a 3-0 victory that also led to the Blades parting company with boss Kevin Blackwell.

Messrs Orr and Helguson were on hand to see off Scunthorpe United in W12, before the R's saved their most spectacular match of the month until last.

Indeed, despite trailing 2-0 going into second-half stoppage-time at Derby County, late, late goals from Patrick Agyemang and Jamie Mackie completed a dramatic last-gasp comeback at Pride Park.

QPR 4, BARNSLEY 0 Loftus Road
npower Championship – Saturday 7th August 2010
Scorers: Helguson (pen 41), Mackie (53), Taarabt (pen 63), Hall (81)
R's Man of the Match: Jamie Mackie

QPR 1, PORT VALE 3 Loftus Road
Carling Cup Round One – Tuesday 10th August 2010
Scorers: QPR – German (62);
Port Vale – Richards (30 & 48), Rigg (36)
R's Man of the Match: Antonio German

SHEFFIELD UNITED 0, QPR 3 Bramall Lane
npower Championship – Saturday 14th August 2010
Scorers: Ephraim (11), Mackie (20), Taarabt (23)
R's Man of the Match: Adel Taarabt

QPR 2, SCUNTHORPE UNITED 0 Loftus Road
npower Championship – Saturday 21st August 2010
Scorers: Orr (17), Helguson (41)
R's Man of the Match: Bradley Orr

DERBY COUNTY 2, QPR 2 Pride Park
npower Championship – Saturday 28th August 2010
Scorers: Derby – Commons (40), Bailey (59);
QPR – Agyemang (90), Mackie (90)
R's Man of the Match: Jamie Mackie

September

The R's juggernaut continued at the start of September, with pre-season title favourites Middlesbrough put to the sword in emphatic style. The match was marred, however, with the loss of Peter Ramage to an Anterior Cruciate Ligament injury.

Man of the moment Jamie Mackie enhanced his ever-growing reputation with a brace at Ipswich Town, on a night when Kyle Walker – the Spurs loanee – made his first start for the R's.

Mackie was at it again with a deadly double to see off Paulo Sousa's Foxes four days later, before Doncaster Rovers were over-powered 3-0 at Loftus Road, thanks to second half goals from Kaspars Gorkss (2) and Adel Taarabt.

Rangers finished the month with a goalless draw at home to London rivals Millwall.

QPR 3, MIDDLESBROUGH 0 Loftus Road
npower Championship – Saturday 11th September 2010
Scorers: Helguson (pen 49), Ephraim (53), Mackie (59)
R's Man of the Match: Hogan Ephraim

IPSWICH TOWN 0, QPR 3 Portman Road
npower Championship – Tuesday 14th September 2010
Scorers: Mackie (31 & 42), Helguson (pen 68)
R's Man of the Match: Jamie Mackie

LEICESTER CITY 0, QPR 2 Walkers Stadium
npower Championship – Saturday 18th September 2010
Scorers: Mackie (12 & 86)
R's Man of the Match: Jamie Mackie

QPR 3, DONCASTER ROVERS 0 Loftus Road
npower Championship – Saturday 25th September 2010
Scorers: Gorkss (53 & 88), Taarabt (81)
R's Man of the Match: Kaspars Gorkss

QPR 0, MILLWALL 0 Loftus Road
npower Championship – Tuesday 28th September 2010
R's Man of the Match: Shaun Derry

October

Rangers returned to Neil Warnock's former Club, Crystal Palace, at the start of October, and what a homecoming it proved to be for the ex-Eagles boss, with Heidar Helguson bagging the R's winner deep into second half stoppage-time.

A goalless draw at home to fellow high-fliers Norwich followed, with Paddy Kenny saving Wes Hoolahan's first half spot-kick, before Patrick Agyemang bagged a late leveller away at Bristol City in front of the live Sky Sports cameras.

Adel Taarabt notched a screamer to open the scoring against Burnley on October 30th, but the ever-reliable Graeme Alexander ensured honours ended even when he fired home from the spot on the stroke of half-time.

CRYSTAL PALACE 1, QPR 2 Selhurst Park
npower Championship – Saturday 3rd October 2010
Scorers: Palace – Cadogan (89); QPR – Taarabt (49), Helguson (90)
R's Man of the Match: Jamie Mackie

QPR 0, NORWICH CITY 0 Loftus Road
npower Championship – Saturday 16th October 2010
R's Man of the Match: Paddy Kenny

SWANSEA CITY 0, QPR 0 Liberty Stadium
npower Championship – Tuesday 19th October 2010
R's Man of the Match: Paddy Kenny

BRISTOL CITY 1, QPR 1 Ashton Gate
npower Championship – Friday 22nd October 2010
Scorers: City – Stead (16); QPR – Agyemang (84)
R's Man of the Match: Alejandro Faurlin

QPR 1, BURNLEY 1 Loftus Road
npower Championship – Saturday 30th October 2010
Scorers: QPR – Taarabt (32); Burnley – Alexander (pen 45)
R's Man of the Match: Adel Taarabt

November

The R's promotion push gathered further momentum at the start of November, as Reading were put to the sword, thanks to goals from Adel Taarabt, Ali Faurlin and Tommy Smith – with Shane Long notching the Royals' reply.

A 1-1 draw at Pompey, in a match where Matt Connolly saw red, added further weight to the cause, with Tommy Smith firing home from the spot in added time.

Rangers drew 0-0 at Forest, before Rob Hulse's first goal of the season and a double from Taarabt helped see off Preston North End in W12.

The month concluded in stunning style for the R's, with Warnock's men coming from behind to beat Cardiff 2-1, with Taarabt's stunning solo goal proving to be the difference.

QPR 3, READING 1 Loftus Road
npower Championship – Saturday 6th November 2010
Scorers: QPR – Taarabt (pen 27), Faurlin (61), Smith (71); Reading – Long (68)
R's Man of the Match: Jamie Mackie

PORTSMOUTH 1, QPR 1 Fratton Park
npower Championship – Tuesday 9th November 2010
Scorers: Pompey – Lawrence (pen 71); Smith (pen 90)
R's Man of the Match: Tommy Smith

NOTTINGHAM FOREST 0, QPR 0 City Ground
npower Championship – Saturday 13th November 2010
R's Man of the Match: Paddy Kenny

QPR 3, PRESTON NORTH END 1 Loftus Road
npower Championship – Saturday 20th November 2010
Scorers: QPR – Hulse (4), Taarabt (56 & 84);
Preston – Connolly (OG 88)
R's Man of the Match: Adel Taarabt

QPR 2, CARDIFF CITY 1 Loftus Road
npower Championship – Saturday 27th November 2010
Scorers: QPR – Gorkss (18), Taarabt (68);
Cardiff – Bellamy (13)
R's Man of the Match: Adel Taarabt

December

Rangers' unbeaten start to the season came to an end against a Watford side who played some splendid stuff at Loftus Road, with in-form striker Danny Graham at the double in the Hornets' 3-1 win.

Max Gradel's double heaped further woe on Warnock's men at Elland Road, but the R's bounced back in superb style on Boxing Day, with Adel Taarabt's stunning second goal – which was later crowned Goal of the Season – seeing off high-flying Swansea City in some fashion at Loftus Road.

The R's concluded their calendar year with a fine 2-0 win at Coventry City in front of the Sky Sports cameras a few days later, with Kyle Walker and Tommy Smith on target.

QPR 1, WATFORD 3 Loftus Road
npower Championship – Friday 10th December 2010
Scorers: QPR – Smith (89); Watford – Graham (26, 48), Mutch (30)
R's Man of the Match: Tommy Smith

Leeds United 2, QPR 0 Elland Road
npower Championship – Saturday 18th December 2010
Scorers: Leeds – Gradel (25, 70)
R's Man of the Match: Shaun Derry

QPR 4, Swansea City 0 Loftus Road
npower Championship – Sunday 26th December 2010
Scorers: QPR – Mackie (16), Helguson (62), Taarabt (79, 80)
R's Man of the Match: Adel Taarabt

Coventry City 0, QPR 2 The Ricoh Arena
npower Championship – Tuesday 28th December 2010
Scorers: QPR – Walker (49), Smith (61)
R's Man of the Match: Kyle Walker

January

The New Year promised to be one to remember for the R's, with Neil Warnock's men sitting pretty at the summit of the npower Championship at the start of 2011.

Things didn't get off to the best of starts, however, with Matt Connolly seeing red in a 1-0 defeat to Norwich on New Year's Day, before Steven Caulker scored deep into second half stoppage-time to salvage a draw for Bristol City a few days later.

And bad turned to worse in the FA Cup at Blackburn Rovers, when a broken leg sustained by Jamie Mackie totally overshadowed a 1-0 defeat to the Premier League side.

A goalless draw at Burnley kick-started the R's recovery, before Wayne Routledge marked his return to the Club with the winner against Coventry City in front of the live Sky Sports cameras.

The month ended with a hard-fought 0-0 draw at ever-improving Hull City.

Norwich City 1, QPR 0
Carrow Road
npower Championship – Saturday 1st January 2011
Scorers: Norwich – Martin (10)
R's Man of the Match: Paddy Kenny

QPR 2, Bristol City 2
Loftus Road
npower Championship – Monday 3rd January 2011
Scorers: QPR – Faurlin (53), Taarabt (85); Bristol City – Pitman (50), Caulker (90)
R's Man of the Match: Alejandro Faurlin

Blackburn Rovers 1, QPR 0
Ewood Park
FA Cup, third round – Saturday 8th January 2011
Scorers: Hoilett (77)
R's Man of the Match: Bruno Andrade

Burnley 0, QPR 0
Turf Moor
npower Championship – Saturday 15th January 2011
R's Man of the Match: Paddy Kenny

QPR 2, Coventry City
Loftus Road
npower Championship – Sunday 23rd January 2011
Scorers: QPR – Taarabt (45), Routledge (79); Coventry – King (25)
R's Man of the Match: Adel Taarabt

Hull City 0, QPR 0
The KC Stadium
npower Championship – Saturday 29th January 2011
R's Man of the Match: Shaun Derry

February

Rangers enjoyed another unbeaten month in February, with Portsmouth the latest side to feel the full force of the R's tilt at the top, thanks to goals from Adel Taarabt and Clint Hill.

The R's left it late to beat Reading on Sky, thanks to Wayne Routledge's 81st minute winner, after Hogan Ephraim had earlier seen red.

Back-to-back 1-1 draws at home to Forest and away at Preston followed, before the Hoops – inspired by Clint Hill – returned to winning ways against Ipswich Town at Loftus Road.

Buoyed by that win, the R's ran riot at Middlesbrough at the end of the month, with Helguson at the double in a 3-0 romp on Teesside.

QPR 2, Portsmouth 0
Loftus Road
npower Championship – Tuesday 1st February 2011
Scorers: QPR – Taarabt (59), Hill (73)
R's Man of the Match: Shaun Derry

Reading 0, QPR 1
The Madejski Stadium
npower Championship – Friday 4th February 2011
Scorers: QPR – Routledge (82)
R's Man of the Match: Alejandro Faurlin

QPR 1, Nottingham Forest 1
Loftus Road
npower Championship – Sunday 13th February 2011
Scorers: QPR – Smith (16); Forest – McGoldrick (26)
R's Man of the Match: Alejandro Faurlin

Preston North End 1, QPR 1
Deepdale
npower Championship – Saturday 19th February 2011
Scorers: PNE – Nicholson (64); QPR – Helguson (37)
R's Man of the Match: Tommy Smith

QPR 2, Ipswich Town 0
Loftus Road
npower Championship – Tuesday 22nd February
Scorers: QPR – Hill (77), Helguson (83)
R's Man of the Match: Clint Hill

Middlesbrough 0, QPR 3
The Riverside Stadium
npower Championship – Saturday 26th February 2011
Scorers: QPR – Helguson (41, 61), Taarabt (68)
R's Man of the Match: Wayne Routledge

March

Three wins and a defeat from four npower Championship fixtures strengthened the R's stranglehold on top spot in the month of March.

Rangers' home fixture against Sven Goran Eriksson's in-form Leicester City appeared to be meandering towards a draw at the start of the month, before the introduction of Ishmael Miller.

The Baggies' loanee scored with his second touch to send Loftus Road wild, only for the R's to succumb to defeat at Millwall three days later, on a night when Danny Shittu saw red for the visitors against his former Club.

Undeterred, Rangers ended March on a high, with wins against Crystal Palace and Doncaster. Heidar Helguson's brace helped see off the ten-man Eagles, before Hogan Ephraim marked his return to the side in the absence of Adel Taarabt with a fine solo goal at The Keepmoat Stadium.

QPR 1, Leicester City 0 Loftus Road
npower Championship – Saturday 5th March 2011
Scorers: QPR – Miller (88)
R's Man of the Match: Ishmael Miller

Millwall 2, QPR 0 The New Den
npower Championship – Tuesday 8th March 2011
Scorers: Millwall – Morison (63), Trotter (73)
R's Man of the Match: Shaun Derry

QPR 2, Crystal Palace 1 Loftus Road
npower Championship – Saturday 12th March 2011
Scorers: QPR – Helguson (20, 54);
Crystal Palace – Vaughan (40)
R's Man of the Match: Heidar Helguson

Doncaster Rovers 0, QPR 1 The Keepmoat Stadium
npower Championship – Saturday 19th March 2011
Scorers: QPR – Ephraim (47)
R's Man of the Match: Hogan Ephraim

April

The month of April proved to be a pivotal one for the R's, who clinched promotion to the Premier League and, with it, the npower Championship title.

Wayne Routledge was at the double to see off struggling Sheffield United at the start of the month, before Rangers were hit for four by Scunthorpe United at Glanford Park.

Undeterred, the R's bounced back to beat Barnsley 1-0 thanks to Adel Taarabt's first minute strike, before three draws on the spin – including a share of the spoils in a four-goal thriller at Cardiff – saw Rangers edge closer to the line.

Promotion and the Championship title was sealed at local rivals Watford, where goals from that man Taarabt and Tommy Smith ended the R's 15 year exile from the top-flight.

QPR 3, Sheffield United 0 Loftus Road
npower Championship – Monday 4th April 2011
Scorers: QPR – Routledge (29, 66), Faurlin (52)
R's Man of the Match: Wayne Routledge

Scunthorpe United 4, QPR 1 Glanford Park
npower Championship – Saturday 9th April 2011
Scorers: Scunthorpe – Garner (28, 48), O'Connor (58),
Duffy (79); QPR – Hulse (7)
R's Man of the Match: The Supporters!

Barnsley 0, QPR 1 Oakwell
npower Championship – Tuesday 12th April 2011
Scorers: QPR – Taarabt (1)
R's Man of the Match: Matt Connolly

QPR 0, Derby County 0 Loftus Road
npower Championship – Monday 18th April 2011
R's Man of the Match: Paddy Kenny

Cardiff City 2, QPR 2 Cardiff City Stadium
npower Championship – Saturday 23rd April 2011
Scorers: Cardiff – Bothroyd (6), Bellamy (35);
QPR –Taarabt (10, 71)
R's Man of the Match: Adel Taarabt

QPR 1, Hull City 1 Loftus Road
npower Championship – Monday 25th April 2011
Scorers: QPR – Routledge (9); Amoo (81)
R's Man of the Match: Alejandro Faurlin

Watford 0, QPR 2 Vicarage Road
npower Championship – Saturday 30th April 2011
Scorers: QPR – Taarabt (77), Smith (90)
R's Man of the Match: Adel Taarabt

May

The R's suffered only their sixth league defeat of the season on the final day of the 2010/11 campaign.

On a day full of emotions for the QPR faithful, Heidar Helguson fired the R's into a first minute lead, only for goals from Max Gradel and Ross McCormack to hand United victory.

QPR 1, Leeds United 2 Loftus Road
Npower Championship – Saturday 7th May 2011
Scorers: QPR – Helguson (1); Leeds – Gradel (38), McCormack (68)
R's Man of the Match: Alejandro Faurlin

We are the Champions

Taarabt's too good for you

Paddy KENNY
Goalkeeper (17-05-78)

Commanding shot-stopper and Republic of Ireland international Paddy Kenny joined QPR in June 2010, penning a three-year deal.

In doing so, the commanding shot-stopper linked up with gaffer Neil Warnock for the third time in his professional career.

Peter RAMAGE
Defender (22-11-83)

A versatile and committed defender, Peter Ramage joined QPR on a free transfer from Newcastle United in the summer of 2008.

The Ashington-born defender - who made 51 starts for his boyhood Club prior to his move to Loftus Road – has made a fine start to life in W12, featuring at right back and centre half in the R's back four.

19

Bradley ORR
Defender (01-11-82)

Cultured defender Bradley Orr joined the R's from Bristol City in the summer of 2010. A pacy right-back who loves to get forward and join the attack at every possible opportunity, Orr's excellent delivery – alongside his defensive qualities – makes him a coveted individual.

Born in Liverpool, the right-back made a total of 42 appearances for City last term, scoring two goals. He is certain to be a key component of Neil Warnock's ever-improving R's side.

Clint HILL
Defender (19-10-78)

Clint Hill – who rose to prominence during a five year spell at Tranmere Rovers, in which time he featured in the 2000 League Cup Final – joined QPR from Crystal Palace on a free transfer in July.

Hill made a total of 126 appearances for the Eagles in a three year spell at Selhurst Park, featuring on 42 occasions in the league last season, as the SE25 outfit narrowly avoided relegation.

Shaun DERRY
Midfielder (16-12-77)

Tough-tackling midfielder Shaun Derry followed Clint Hill across London this summer, penning a contract following a successful spell as skipper at Crystal Palace.

Derry made 129 outings in his second spell south of the capital, skippering the Eagles to safety in difficult circumstances last season after Palace were placed into administration, and with it suffered a ten-point deduction.

Fitz HALL
Defender (20-12-80)

Fitz Hall penned a four-and-a-half year deal with Rangers at the start of the 2008 January transfer window and was handed the captain's armband at the start of this season.

The defender - who gained vast Premiership experience during spells at Wigan Athletic and Crystal Palace - spent time on loan at Newcastle United last season, but is regarded by Neil Warnock as 'one of the best defender's in this division.'

Mikele LEIGERTWOOD
Midfielder (12-11-82)

Rangers completed the signing of no-nonsense midfielder Mikele Leigertwood on the final day of the 2007 summer transfer window.

The former Sheffield United ace has been a key player for the R's since then, skippering the side on a number of occasions in the heart of the Rangers midfield.

Adel TAARABT
Midfielder (24-05-89)

Rangers clinched the coveted signing of Adel Taarabt on the eve of the 2010/11 npower Championship campaign.

R's gaffer Neil Warnock pulled off one of the master-strokes of the summer by moving for the Spurs midfield man, who had previously enjoyed two memorable loan spells in West London.

Akos BUZSAKY
Midfielder (07-05-82)

A player with outstanding individual ability, Akos Buzsaky made an immediate impact following his permanent move to W12 from fellow Championship outfit Plymouth Argyle in January 2008.

The Hungarian international, who initially joined on loan prior to making the deal permanent, scored six goals in his first 13 appearances, and ended the campaign with ten goals to his name.

Buzsaky's taste for the spectacular also saw him scoop the Kiyan Prince Goal of the Season.

Jamie MACKIE
Midfielder (22-09-85)

Jamie Mackie joined QPR in the summer of 2010 following Plymouth Argyle's relegation to League One.

The hardworking, yet equally talented attacker, was the stand-out performer for the Home Park outfit last season, notching eight goals in all competitions.

Leon CLARKE
Striker (10-02-85)

A product of the Wolverhampton Wanderers academy, Leon Clarke joined the Rangers revolution in the summer following his release from Sheffield Wednesday.

Clarke notched six goals in all competitions last season, but his efforts weren't quite enough to keep Alan Irvine's side in the second tier, as the Owls were relegated on the final day of the campaign.

Patrick AGYEMANG
Striker (29-09-80)

Patrick Agyemang joined QPR from Preston in January 2008 on a four-and-a-half year deal, after the two Clubs agreed an undisclosed fee for his services.

The Ghanaian international enjoyed a honeymoon period to remember for the R's, bagging eight goals in his first six league appearances.

Agyemang went on to score nine goals in all competitions, only for injuries to halt his progress in W12.

Kaspars GORKSS
Defender (06-11-81)

Rangers ended their search for a centre half with the capture of Kaspars Gorkss in July 2008.

The Latvian international put pen to paper on a three year deal, after the R's agreed an undisclosed fee with Blackpool for his services.

And the giant defender – after a mixed start to life in W12 – went on to enjoy a profitable maiden season at Loftus Road, making 35 appearances in all competitions, and finishing runner-up in both the Players' Player and Supporters' Player of the Year awards.

Martin ROWLANDS
Midfielder (08-02-79)

Hammersmith-born midfielder Martin Rowlands joined Rangers in July 2003 on a free transfer from local rivals Brentford.

An outstanding 2007/08 campaign saw the midfielder named Players' Player of the Year and, after a four-year absence from the international fold, Rowlands was recalled to the full Republic of Ireland squad under new Eire boss Giovanni Trapattoni.

But his 2009/10 campaign failed to hit such heights, with an Anterior Cruciate Ligament injury ending his season prematurely.

PLAYER**PROFILES**

Matthew CONNOLLY
Defender (24-09-87)

Matthew Connolly penned a three-and-a-half year deal with the R's in January 2008.

A product of the successful Arsenal academy, Connolly has since gone on to feature regularly for the R's and is regarded as one of the hottest talents outside of the top-flight.

Lee COOK
Midfielder (03-08-82)

R's fans' favourite Lee Cook rejoined Rangers on loan from Fulham in August 2008.

The left sided midfielder, who joined the Cottagers just 12 months earlier, was named both Players' Player and Supporters' Player of the Year prior to his departure to the West London outfit.

But an injury-interrupted spell at Craven Cottage eventually led to his return to W12, and after making his loan deal permanent in January 2009, Cook went on to make 38 appearances in all competitions in his first season back at Loftus Road.

Radek CERNY
Goalkeeper (18-02-74)

Goalkeeper Radek Cerny joined the R's in the summer of 2008.

The former Tottenham Hotspur and Slavia Prague stopper arrived in W12 with a terrific track record and duly went on to make the number one jersey his own.

Cerny was a mainstay in the R's side throughout the 2008/09 campaign, making 47 appearances in all competitions, and inspiring Rangers to achieve one of the best defensive records in the Championship.

He is currently competing with Paddy Kenny for the R's number one jersey.

Hogan EPHRAIM
Midfielder (31-03-88)

After a successful loan spell in W12, winger Hogan Ephraim signed a three-and-a-half year contract with QPR in January 2008.

The diminutive winger made 30 appearances in all competitions in 2007/08, scoring two goals, and proved what a valuable, versatile asset he is to the R's side again last term.

The midfielder scored a stunning third goal in our 3-0 demolition of Blackpool, as the former England Youth product excelled in a more central role.

He had since go on to prove his undoubted worth for the Club, playing in a variety of positions.

Heidar HELGUSON
Striker (22-08-77)

QPR rescued Iceland international Helguson from Bolton Wanderers after the former Watford man fell out of favour under then-Manager Gary Megson.

Initially signed on a loan deal, he made the move to W12 permanent as soon as the transfer window opened in January 2009.

Three goals in seven appearances indicated a man relieved to be back playing, and he has added a new dimension to the Rangers attack with tireless work rate and phenomenal aerial prowess.

Gary BORROWDALE
Defender (16-07-85)

Former England Under-21 defender Gary Borrowdale joined the R's from Coventry City in January 2009.

However, his appearances have been restricted since then, and he's spent time on loan at both Brighton & Hove Albion and Charlton Athletic.

Alejandro FAURLIN
Midfielder (09-08-86)

Argentine midfielder Alejandro Faurlin penned a three year deal in the summer of 2009.

Faurlin's impact was immediate, as he went on to win the Players' Player and Supporters' Player of the Year awards in his first full season at the Club.

Rob HULSE
Striker (25-10-79)

Rangers completed the signing of Rob Hulse from Derby County in the final hours of the summer transfer window.

The former Leeds United and Sheffield United front-man penned a three year deal at Loftus Road.

Tommy SMITH
Striker (22-05-80)

QPR swooped to bring Tommy Smith to the Club on loan in early September.

The livewire front-man, who has extensive experience in both the Premier League and the Championship, signed a permanent contract when the transfer window re-opened in January.

WORDSEARCH

Find the players' names in the grid. Words can go horizontally, vertically and diagonally in all eight directions.

X	Y	N	O	S	U	G	L	E	H	M	N	M	H
L	N	P	G	O	R	K	S	S	I	T	H	Y	A
K	N	T	H	T	I	M	S	A	C	U	A	N	L
K	E	T	N	B	C	C	R	K	L	K	G	R	L
R	K	R	N	J	T	H	W	S	M	G	Y	E	L
L	R	V	M	Y	P	F	E	Q	Q	V	E	C	N
O	X	K	C	E	K	H	I	L	L	M	M	T	I
E	G	D	P	O	E	A	L	Y	N	R	A	R	L
F	G	W	E	I	N	K	Z	Y	N	A	N	B	R
K	Z	A	K	R	Q	N	W	S	R	W	G	Z	U
T	H	C	M	J	R	Y	O	A	U	G	L	P	A
M	A	W	T	A	G	Y	B	L	Y	B	N	K	F
M	B	Q	N	D	R	T	T	P	L	L	M	Q	N
R	O	U	T	L	E	D	G	E	R	Y	N	T	L

Agyemang	**Buzsaky**	**Cerny**
Connolly	**Derry**	**Ephraim**
Faurlin	**Gorkss**	**Hall**
Helguson	**Hill**	**Hulse**
Kenny	**Mackie**	**Orr**
Ramage	**Routledge**	**Smith**
Taarabt		

Answers on page 61

King Kenny
Player of the Year

Paddy Kenny reigned supreme at the R's Player of the Year event.

The Rangers number one scooped the prestigious Players' Player of the Year accolade, as well as winning the Supporters' Player of the Year crown at a star-studded West London event.

The awards double capped a quite remarkable maiden season in W12 for the former Sheffield United keeper, who was also named in the PFA's Championship Team of the Year.

npower Championship Player of the Year Adel Taarabt clinched the Kiyan Prince Goal of the Season award for his stunning solo goal against Swansea City on Boxing Day.

Meanwhile, midfield general Shaun Derry featured prominently, finishing second runner-up in the Supporters' Player of the Year behind Taarabt and overall winner Kenny.

Young prospect Bruno Andrade was named Daphne Biggs Supporters' Young Player of the Year, whilst elsewhere, R's fan Ian Stenning scooped the Supporter of the Year accolade and R's defender Peter Ramage won the QPR Community Award for his outstanding commitment to community projects throughout the campaign.

Congratulations to all the winners!

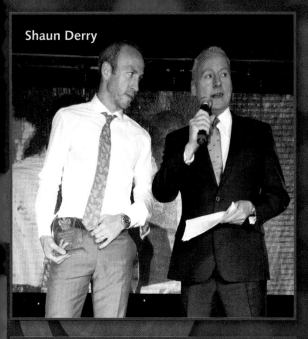
Shaun Derry

Bruno Andrade

Adel Taarabt

Roll of Honour

Supporters' Player of the Year
Paddy Kenny

Supporters' Player of the Year 1st Runner up
Adel Taarabt

Supporters' Player of the Year 2nd Runner up
Shaun Derry

Ray Jones Players' Player of the Year
Paddy Kenny

Daphne Biggs Supporters'
Young Player of the Year
Bruno Andrade

Kiyan Prince Goal of the Season
Adel Taarabt
(second goal v Swansea City)

Supporter of the Year
Ian Stenning

QPR Community Award
(for outstanding commitment to community
projects season 2010/11)
Peter Ramage

GOALS GALORE

GOALS **GALORE**

A NEW ERA

QUEENS PARK RANGERS
LOFTUS ROAD · LONDON · 1882

Malaysian business tycoon Tony Fernandes CBE completed his takeover of Queens Park Rangers Football Club on Thursday 18th August.

Fernandes' company Tune Group bought a majority stake in the Club, buying out previous majority shareholders Flavio Briatore and Bernie Ecclestone.

The 47 year-old founder of AirAsia, who is also the team principal of Formula One's Team Lotus, and his business partners, bought a controlling stake of 66 per-cent, working alongside the Mittal Family, who retained their 33 per-cent stake.

Speaking exclusively to www.qpr.co.uk, Fernandes said: "I lived in Uxbridge Road for many years and grew up around the area.

Everyone knows I've followed West Ham all my life, but I've always had a soft spot for QPR.

Rangers were one of the first teams I watched as a child at Loftus Road."

Fernandes took the role of Chairman of QPR Holdings Ltd and was joined on the board by joint Tune Group owner Mr Kamarudin Bin Meranun, one of Malaysia's most successful business tycoons.

He added: "The opportunity to get involved with the Club was mentioned to me by the previous owners and here I am.

I've always wanted to be involved in football and the appeal of a London Club, like QPR, was too good an opportunity to turn down.

It's funny how life has a way of spinning things round. It goes full circle sometimes.

QPR is a raw diamond and hopefully I can contribute into turning it into a diamond."

Amit Bhatia, who resumed his position as Vice Chairman of the Club, told www.qpr.co.uk: "I'm very excited to welcome Tony to QPR and having spent considerable time with him, know that we share the same vision and values.

We have discussed in great detail how to restore pride at the Club and I'm very pleased with the outcome of these discussions.

QUEENS PARK RANGERS

It was a very difficult decision to resign from the board when I did, so I'm thrilled to be back and I would like to thank all those who supported me and my family and look forward to serving the Club to the best of my abilities again.

Tony and I will work alongside each other to try and make this season as exciting and successful as possible. I love this Club and this is a very happy day for me."

Fernandes added: "I have ambitions in the long term.

I could easily say we're going to win the Champions League and the Premier League, but that's really not my style. I don't want to make big promises I can't guarantee.

I want the fans to be proud of what we're doing and be involved as much as we can. The fans pay good money and are stakeholders, so whatever we do, I want the fans to be proud. We'll do it in style and with integrity.

I'm keen to create a good Academy, so that there's a constant supply of players. We're in a fantastic part of London and we should be bringing kids through.

The third aspect is to be a strong partner in the community and to make a difference in the community.

Of course you don't go into anything in the sporting world and not want to be the best, but these things take time and I'd rather let the results speaks for themselves."

We are the Champions

Alejandro Faurlin

There's only one Paddy Kenny

WHOSE BOOTS?

Can you match the boots to the player?

1

2

3

4

5

6

Answers on page 60

A hard hitting Shaun Derry

JAY'S PREMIER GOAL

Exclusive Interview by *Ian Taylor*

Whilst Adel Taarabt took the plaudits at Loftus Road last year, 150 miles down the road in Cardiff, Jay Bothroyd was writing his own headlines.

Twenty goals in 42 appearances earned him a call-up to Fabio Capello's Three Lions squad – and with it, national acclaim for a career that looked doomed when a flash of ill-temper when he was a teenager saw him ditched by Arsenal before he'd even kicked a ball in anguish.

Bothroyd was one of the stand-out figures in the second tier last season, as Cardiff City fell just short in their bid to join the R's at the top table of English football.

Out of contract at the end of the campaign and with numerous offers on the table, Bothroyd eventually plumped for a move to QPR, becoming the first full current England international to sign for the Hoops since Tony Currie in 1979.

"I had a lot of options," he said.

"When I was with Cardiff I was fully focused over the last six months or so of my time there in helping the Club gain promotion to the Premier League.

"Obviously it wasn't to be and it was a case of me wanting to play in the Premier League.

"I want to test myself week in, week out and be amongst that pool of players that are under the spotlight every week.

"I want to get back in the national team again and whilst I proved it can be done by playing in the Championship, the Premier League is the place to showcase your talents.

"I've come here with a different mind-set to when I last played in the Premier League and I'm so hungry and determined to do well for QPR."

A lot of factors contributed towards Bothroyd's decision to move to W12, as he explained: "As a footballer you want to improve every day and I feel as though I can do that here.

"I'm from London and my son lives in London, so this was always an attractive proposition for me.

"There was a lot of thought behind it, but after speaking to Neil Warnock he convinced me that this is the right place for me."

Despite hitting such heady heights last season, Bothroyd insists he's not about to rest on his laurels.

"Last season means nothing now – for me or QPR," he said.

"I achieved at Championship level by scoring 20 goals last season – and QPR went up as Champions.

"But that's in the past now. That was all at Championship level. The Premier League is a different level altogether.

"This is a big season for me and QPR now.

"I've got a lot to prove to myself and any doubters that there are out there."

WHO DUNNIT?

Can you name the QPR players who scored these goals?

1 An unbelievable bicycle kick from the edge of the area against Barnsley in the FA Cup in 1997

2 After chesting the ball down from Radek Cerny's goal-kick, he jinked his way past three Preston players before finding the top corner from 20 yards.

3 We're 2-0 down at Derby and time's running out. Patrick Agyemang pulls a goal back before this man levelled with a fantastic goal deep in injury time to preserve our unbeaten start to the current campaign!

4 After an excellent London derby, the game seemed to be heading for a 1-1 draw at Crystal Palace before Tommy Smith saw which player head home his cross for a late, late winner?

5 At Coventry City last season, we're 1-0 up before this man scores with a clever header following Adel Taaarabt's perfect delivery

Answers on page 61

A KIT OF ALRIGHT

QPR donned their new home kit for the 2011/12 season in our opening day Barclays Premier League clash with Bolton Wanderers.

The strip was designed and manufactured by Lotto Sport Italia - QPR's Technical Sponsor and Official Kit Supplier since 2008 – with both Lotto and the Club working in close collaboration to produce the R's new home jersey.

From a stylistic point of view, the kit perfectly represents the Club's tradition and history thanks to the continuous reflex blue and white horizontal hoops.

The back of the collar hosts the commemorative embroidery of the 125 years since the Club's formation in 1886, when St. Jude's Institute merged with Christ Church Rangers.

The final part of the sleeves is enriched by an elegant silver piping and the Club's emblem is presented on the chest in a high definition patch.

The home kit's shorts are all-white and enriched by the Club's emblem on the front part and by the double diamond on both lateral sides.

From a functional point of view, the kit combines lightness and breathability with a comfortable and ergonomic fit thanks to the Poly Double Mesh 10, an elasticated fabric ideal even in the most challenging phases of the game.

As per Lotto's tradition, there's also great attention to detail. The England flag sits inside of the shirt and the Club's emblem is processed with Lextra, which offers a special 3D effect.

SPOT THE BALL

Can you guess which ball is in the correct spot?

Answers on page 60

GOAL of the Season

QPR scored some quite sensational goals during the 2010/11 npower Championship campaign, as Neil Warnock's men surged to the league title.

Ten strikes in total were nominated on to the shortlist – whilst many great goals missed out, which makes you realise how many wonder goals the R's scored last term!

The shortlist was as follows:

GOAL A

Heidar Helguson v Scunthorpe (h) 21st August

GOAL B

Jamie Mackie v Derby (a) 28th August

GOAL C

Hogan Ephraim v Middlesbrough (h) 11th September

Jamie Mackie v Leicester (a) 18th September

GOAL D

GOAL E

Adel Taarabt v Burnley (h) 30th October

GOAL F

Adel Taarabt v Cardiff (h) 27th November

GOAL G

**Adel Taarabt's second
v Swansea (h)
26th December**

GOAL H

Wayne Routledge v Coventry (h) 22nd January

GOAL I

Heidar Helguson
v Middlesbrough (a)
26th February

GOAL of the Season

The nominations came in by the bucket load, yet there was one stand-out winner when the deadline closed a fortnight prior to our annual Player of the Year event.

Adel Taarabt's stunning solo goal against Swansea City on Boxing Day was the cream of the crop, with the magical Moroccan on hand to pick up his award at the end of season showcase in London.

Picking the ball up on the left flank, Taarabt played a neat one-two with Kyle Walker, before nutmegging Joe Allen.

With the Swans midfield all at seas, Taarabt moved into the space he created and curled a delicious strike into the far right hand corner of the net, giving Swans custodian Dorus De Vries absolutely no chance.

Take a bow son!

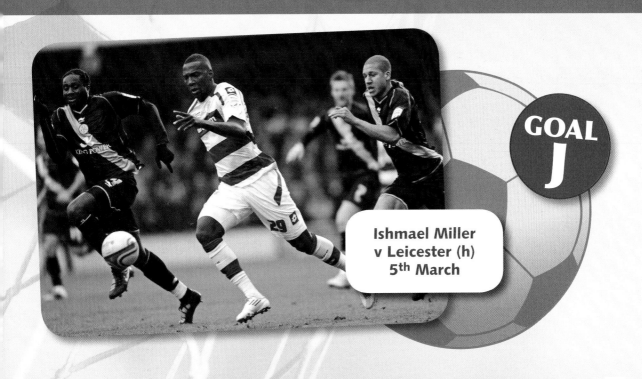

GOAL J

Ishmael Miller
v Leicester (h)
5th March

SPOT THE DIFFERENCE

Can you spot 6 differences between the two pictures below?

Answers on page 60

Tommy Smith

Back to Work

No rest for the team, it's time to hit the ground running with some essential pre-season training at Harlington.

Trophy Time

QPR FIXTURES 2011-12 SEASON

Date	Kick-off	Opponent	Home/ Away	Competition	TV
August 2011					
Saturday 13 August	15.00	Bolton Wanderers	Home	Premier League	
Saturday 20 August	15.00	Everton	Away	Premier League	
Tuesday 23 August	19.45	Rochdale	Home	Carling Cup	
Saturday 27 August	12.30	Wigan Athletic	Away	Premier League	
September 2011					
Monday 12 September	20.00	Newcastle Utd	Home	Premier League	SKY
Saturday 17 September	15.00	Wolverhampton Wanderers	Away	Premier League	
Sunday 25 September	16.00	Aston Villa	Home	Premier League	SKY
October 2011					
Saturday 1 Oct	15.00	Fulham	Away	Premier League	
Saturday 15 Oct	15.00	Blackburn Rovers	Home	Premier League	
Sunday 23rd October	16.00	Chelsea	Home	Premier League	SKY
Saturday 29 Oct	16.00	Tottenham Hotspur	Away	Premier League	SKY
November 2011					
Saturday 5 November	17.30	Manchester City	Home	Premier League	ESPN
Saturday 19 November	15.00	Stoke City	Away	Premier League	
Saturday 26 November	15.00	Norwich City	Away	Premier League	
December 2011					
Saturday 3 December	15.00	West Bromwich Albion	Home		
Saturday 10 December	15.00	Liverpool	Away	Premier League	
Saturday 17 December	15.00	Manchester United	Home	Premier League	
Tuesday 20 December	20.00	Sunderland	Home	Premier League	
Monday 26 December	15.00	Swansea City	Away	Premier League	
Saturday 31 December	15.00	Arsenal	Away	Premier League	
January 2012					
Monday 2 January	15.00	Norwich City	Home	Premier League	
Saturday 14 January	15.00	Newcastle Utd	Away	Premier League	
Saturday 21 January	15.00	Wigan Athletic	Home	Premier League	
February 2012					
Wednesday 1 February	19.45	Aston Villa	Away	Premier League	
Saturday 4th February	15.00	Wolverhampton Wanderers	Home	Premier League	
Saturday 11 February	15.00	Blackburn Rovers	Away	Premier League	
Saturday 25 February	15.00	Fulham	Home	Premier League	
March 2012					
Saturday 3 March	15.00	Everton	Home	Premier League	
Saturday 10 March	15.00	Bolton Wanderers	Away	Premier League	
Saturday 17 March	15.00	Liverpool	Home	Premier League	
Saturday 24 March	15.00	Sunderland	Away		
Saturday 31 March	15.00	Arsenal	Home	Premier League	
April 2012					
Saturday 7 April	15.00	Manchester United	Away	Premier League	
Monday 9 April	15.00	Swansea City	Home	Premier League	
Saturday 14 April	15.00	West Bromwich Albion	Away	Premier League	
Saturday 21 April	15.00	Tottenham Hotspur	Home	Premier League	
Saturday 28 April	15.00	Chelsea	Away	Premier League	
May 2012					
Saturday 5 May	15.00	Stoke City	Home	Premier League	
Sunday 13 May	15.00	Manchester City	Away	Premier League	

WORDSEARCH

Find the stadium names in the grid. Words can go horizontally, vertically and diagonally in all eight directions.

Q	G	T	K	K	B	Q	K	V	L	H	Z	K	N
E	G	D	I	R	B	D	R	O	F	M	A	T	S
K	T	K	Q	R	C	K	D	M	V	L	K	V	P
R	C	R	D	E	M	I	R	A	T	E	S	D	O
A	A	A	T	A	N	N	Q	F	C	K	A	T	L
P	N	P	E	P	O	T	M	J	V	O	N	M	D
S	F	N	Z	W	G	R	L	N	R	N	O	D	T
E	I	O	B	W	O	N	W	S	X	L	P	X	R
M	E	S	V	C	V	O	U	O	I	Z	V	X	A
A	L	I	Y	J	C	T	D	N	R	Z	V	H	F
J	D	D	H	Z	F	K	E	P	K	R	J	V	F
T	Z	O	N	O	W	U	Q	N	A	P	A	W	O
S	H	O	L	M	X	L	V	Y	L	R	Q	C	R
H	N	G	K	L	N	X	R	L	K	K	K	T	D

Anfield

Carrow Road

Emirates

Ewood Park

Goodison Park

Loftus Road

Molineux

Old Trafford

Stamford Bridge

St James Park

Wordsearch answers on page 61. Superhoops Quiz answers on page 60.

SUPERHOOPS QUIZ

1. Who were the only team to do the double over the R'S?

2. Which team were the first to beat QPR in the league?

3. How many goals were conceded in the league?

4. Name the two goal scorers with late goals to earn a draw at Pride Park?

5. Who was the highest goal scorer?

6. How many away games did QPR win?

7. Which defender plays in the number 13 shirt?

8. Which player was loaned out to Reading?

9. Name the 3 players who made the most appearances in the 2010/11 season?

10. What was the score in our Carling cup defeat to Port Vale?

23. On which date did QPR suffer their first away defeat?

24. From which Premier League Club did we sign Wayne Routledge on loan from?

13. Who scored the injury time winner against Crystal Palace at Selhurst Park?

14. Who were the opponents in our lowest crowd attendance at home?

15. Which player received the most red cards and how many did he get?

16. Former Fulham midfielder made his only appearance of the season at Blackburn in the F.A Cup?

17. Most fouls committed by which QPR player?

18. Former R's defender who returned to Loftus Road in the latter half of the season?

19. How many goals did Alejandro Faurlin score in the league?

20. Wears the number 19 shirt?

21. Who started the season as captain and wears the number 5 shirt?

22. How many clean sheets did Paddy Kenny keep?

23. What was the score in our opening day fixture at home to Barnsley?

24. Which number 7 had the most shots on target for QPR?

Quiz Answers

Page 40 – Whose Boots?

1. Akos Buzsaky
2. Clint Hill
3. Alejandro Faurlin
4. Fitz Hall
5. Heidar Helguson
6. Hogan Ephraim

Page 43 – Who Dunnit?

1. Trevor Sinclair, 2. Adel Taarabt, 3. Jamie Mackie, 4. Heidar Helguson, 5. Tommy Smith

Page 47 – Spot the Ball

Page 52 – Spot the Difference

Page 59 – Superhoops Quiz

1. Leeds
2. Watford
3. 32
4. Jamie Mackie & Patrick Agyemang
5. Adel Taarabt
6. 9
7. Kaspars Gorkss
8. Mikele Leigertwood
9. Paddy Kenny, Shaun Derry & Clint Hill
10. 3-1 Port Vale
11. Saturday 18th December 2010
12. Newcastle
13. Heider Helguson
14. Scunthorpe
15. Matthew Connolly 2
16. Lee Cook
17. Clint Hill
18. Danny Shittu
19. 3
20. Patrick Agyemang
21. Fitz Hall
22. 24
23. 4-0 QPR
24. Adel Taarabt

Page 27 – Wordsearch (players)

```
X Y N O S U G L E H M N M H
L N P G O R K S S I T H Y A
K N T H T I M S A C U A N L
K E T N B C C R K L K G R L
R K R N J T H W S M G Y E L
L R V M Y P F E Q Q V E C N
O X K C E K H I L L M M T I
E G D P O E A L Y N R A R L
F G W E I N K Z Y N A N B R
K Z A K R Q N W S R W G Z U
T H C M J R Y O A U G L P A
M A W T A G Y B L Y B N K F
M B Q N D R T T P L L M Q N
R O U T L E D G E R Y N T L
```

Page 58 – Wordsearch (stadiums)

```
Q G T K K B Q K V L H Z K N
E G D I R B D R O F M A T S
K T K Q R C K D M V L K V P
R C R D E M I R A T E S D O
A A A T A N N Q F C K A T L
P N P E P O T M J V O N M D
S F N Z W G R L N R N O D T
E I O B W O N W S X L P X R
M E S V C V O U O I Z X A
A L I Y J C T D N R Z V H F
J D D H Z F K E P K R J V F
T Z O N O W U Q N A P A W O
S H O L M X L V Y L R Q C R
H N G K L N X R L K K K T D
```

WHERE'S SPARK?